Someone's Perfect Poo
by Doctor Cannell

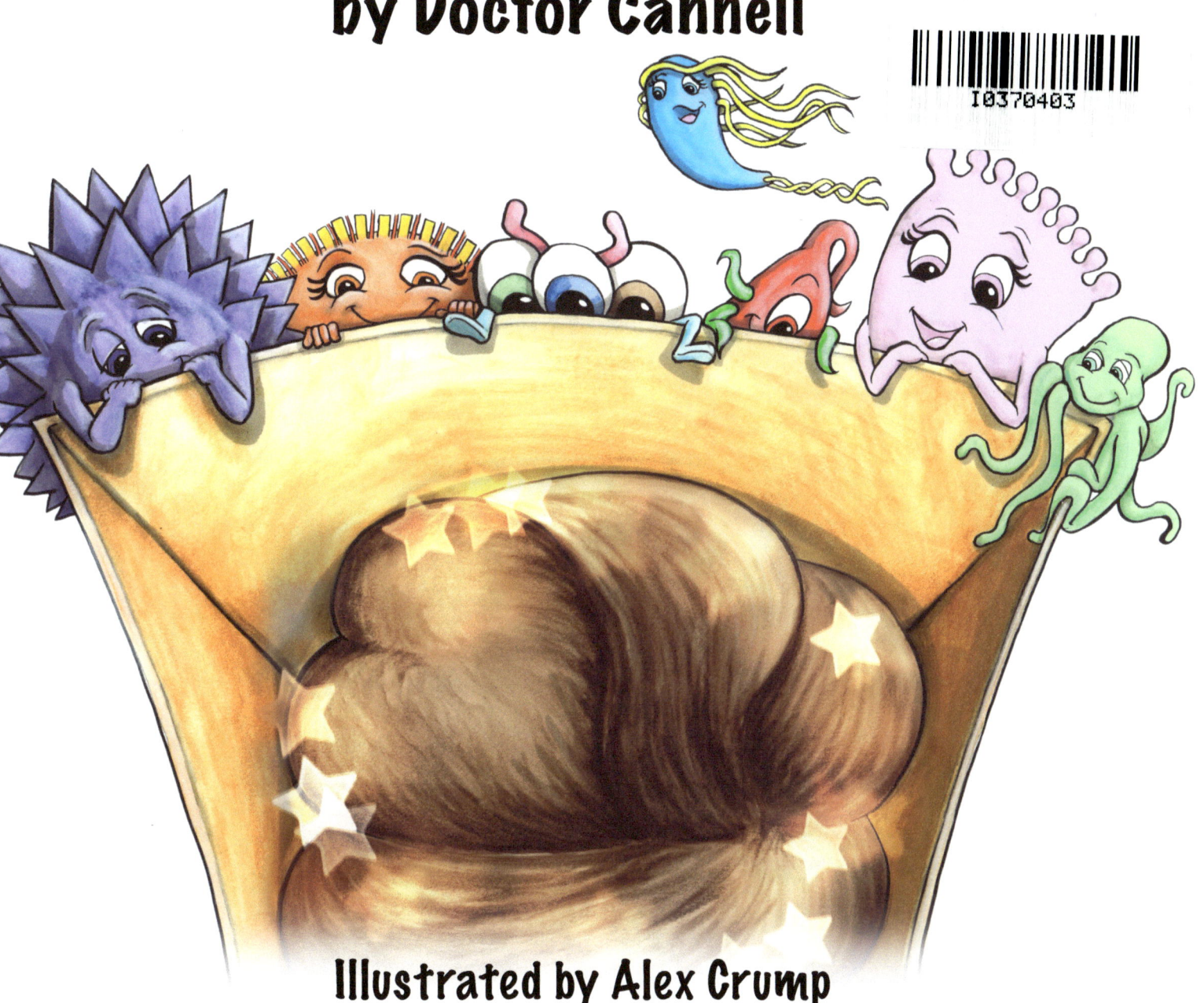

Illustrated by Alex Crump

© 2023 Doctor Felicity Cannell - Author
© 2023 Alex Crump - Illustrator

ISBN: 978 1 7384108 0 4

All rights reserved. No part of this publication may be reproduced, distributed, or transmitted in any form or by any means, including photocopying, recording, or other electronic or mechanical methods, without the prior written permission of the publisher, except in the case of brief quotations embodied in critical reviews and certain other noncommercial uses permitted by copyright law.

First Edition 2023

Someone's Perfect Poo
by Doctor Cannell

Illustrated by Alex Crump

The Poobugs!

They are not just your friends. They are everybody's friends.
And Someone's friends. They live in the Tunnel of Been, deep down inside
Someone's tummy, and work hard, all day, every day, to make poo.

No-one knows why it's called the Tunnel of Been. It may be because back when Someone
sat on the potty Pops used to shout 'have you Been yet?'
Or maybe it's because all the poo has Been something else.
Some way or another the name stuck.

But that's enough introductions and pleasant chat passing the time of day.
The Poobugs want to get back to work, because work is what they like doing best.

The Poobugs are in charge of Leftovers. That might not sound like fun.
If you were sitting at the table and had to wait for everyone else to finish their dinner before you could eat what's left, you might be a bit cross, but the Poobugs love it!
They taste every last morsel to make sure nothing good gets missed,
because by the time dinner gets to the Tunnel of Been a carrot and a chocolate bar look very much the same.

Liliashus finds the leftover bits of vegetables and fruit, then chops them into tiny chunks.

Prevotella bangs and bashes the leftover gristly parts of meat, chewy skins of sweetcorn, seeds and nuts.

Then Acidophilus packages up what's been found and posts it all around your body.

Baxter pushes the rest along the tunnel and shovels it into the poo processor.

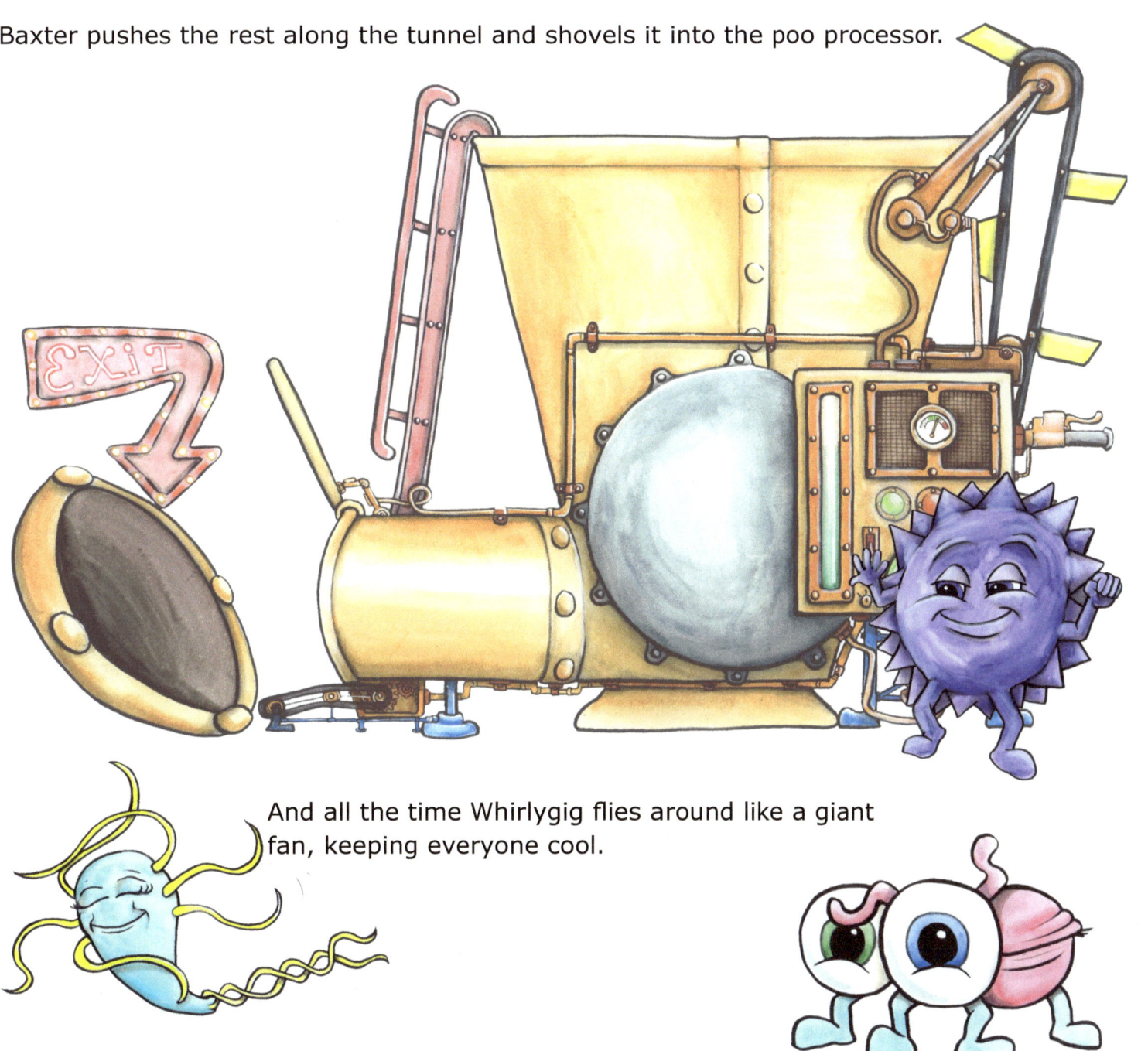

And all the time Whirlygig flies around like a giant fan, keeping everyone cool.

Ruminoco is the tunnel policeman. He's in charge of looking out for the bad guys. (But that's a story for another day)

Working hard is called 'getting stuck into something', and the Poobugs certainly like to get stuck into the hard stuff.

Whenever Someone leaves the crust of a jam sandwich on the side of the plate Acidophilus hops up and down in fury.
That's one of the best bits for the Poobugs.

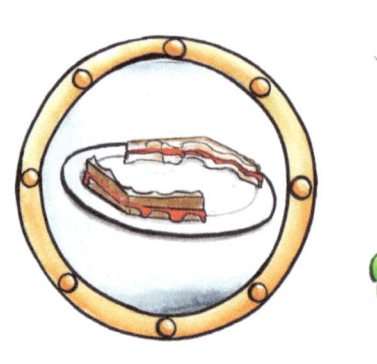

'Rough, tough, chewy stuff. We can never get enough!' they shout down the line to each other.

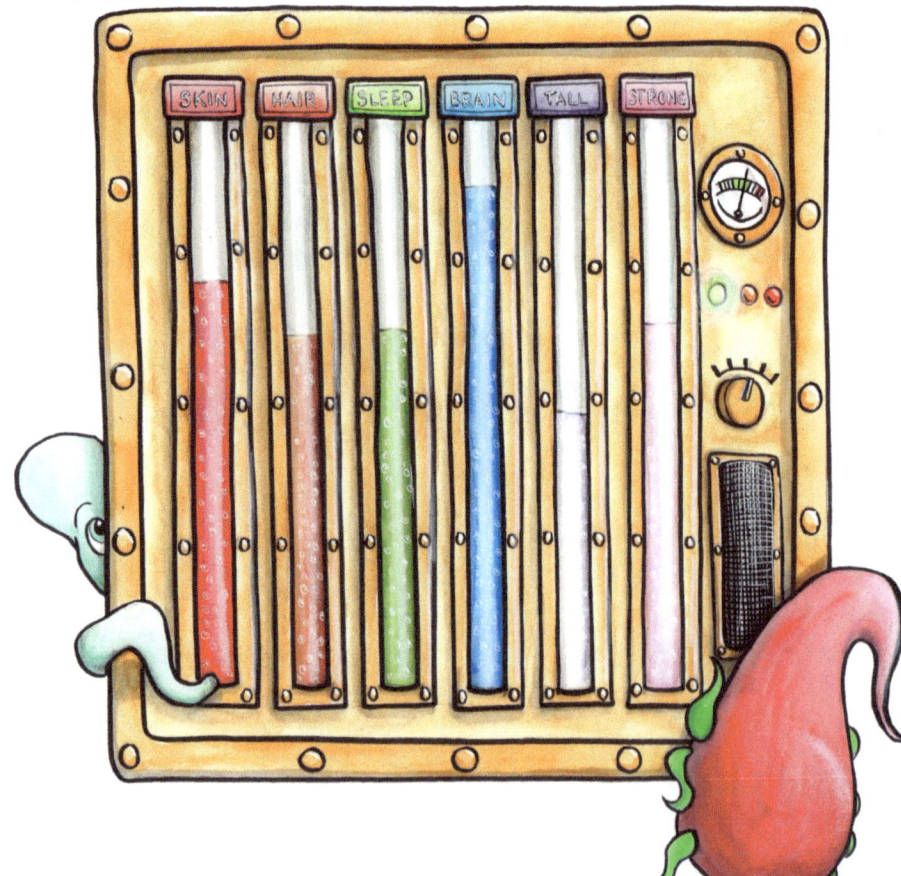

The Poobugs dig out bits to make your skin glow and your hair shiny, to make you sleep well and remember your times tables the next day.

The Poobugs send them here, there, and everywhere around your body, making you taller and stronger.

And cleverer.

Some bits of fish, for instance, get sent to make your brain bigger!

So you really are what you eat.

You know that nursery rhyme about little boys and girls? Little boys are made of slugs and snails (yuk!!) and little girls are made of sugar and spice (yummy!!). But actually, slugs and snails are MUCH better for you than sugar and spice so don't take any notice of that!

But today was a BAD poo day. Someone had been to a party and eaten far too many sweets. Jelly beans and fruit gums, sticky toffee and chocolate buttons, lollipops and liquorice.
Someone had eaten far too many sweets and NOTHING ELSE!

Baxter turned the handle of the poo processor. It groaned and clanged. It creaked and shuddered. And then it stopped. The poo was so hard and lumpy the poo processor was stuck fast. Baxter pushed and pushed. He heaved and ho-ed. First with one shoulder, and then the other.

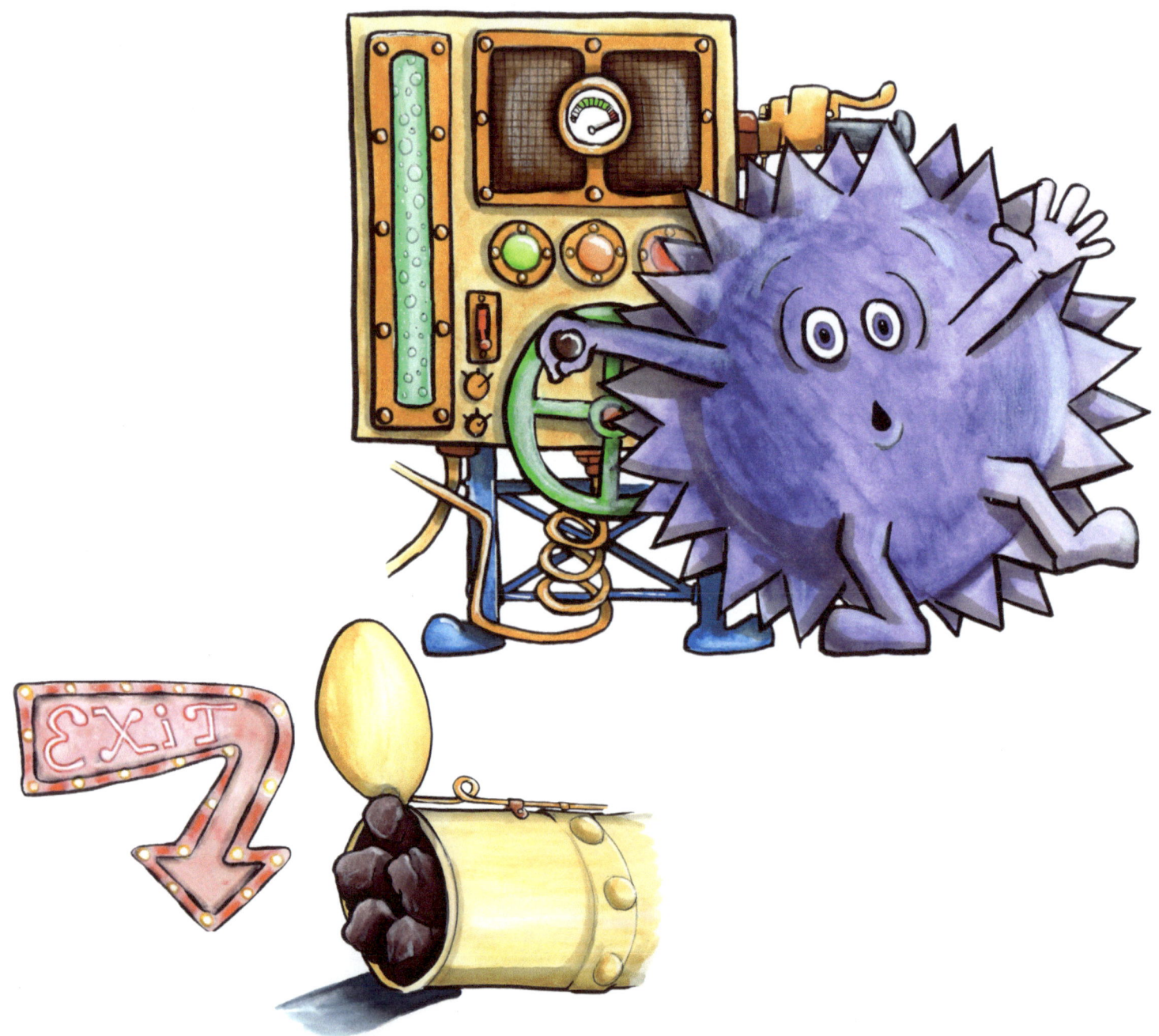

"Put your back into it!" shouted Whirlygig, which generally means try harder. But Baxter did just that. He turned round, sat down, bent his knees and pushed backwards as hard as he could.

Little by little the poo moved.
Pop! One lump shot out.
Two lumps…….
Three lumps…….
Phew!

Poo should be soft and squishy, not hard and lumpy.

Making a poo is a bit like making a cake. What goes into the mixing bowl makes all the difference to whether you have a nice fluffy, moist, creamy sponge cake, or a
nasty, dry, heavy slab which sticks to the roof of your mouth.

The best poo is made from a little bit of this and a little bit of that. And a little bit of the other. That means many different ingredients, different types of food, even different colours.

Have you ever wondered why poo is brown?

Poo is brown because, just like your paintbox, if you mix everything together – red, yellow, black, blue, green and purple, orange and grey – it always ends up brown.

Light brown or dark brown, but always brown.

What you eat is like your box of paints: red tomatoes, bright green peas, white potatoes, purple beetroot, orange carrots, yellow sweetcorn, pink fizzy drink and blueberry jam.

Mush it all up for several hours (because that's how long the Poobugs like to take) and it all turns brown.

Now too many sweets don't just make dry, heavy rocks of poo.

Too many sweets also make you very thirsty.

Someone woke up the next morning, headed for the fridge and grabbed a large carton of apple juice.
Of course, apples are good for you.

"An apple a day keeps the doctor away" sings Liliashus, as often as anyone will listen to her.

Even eating two apples is just fine. But a carton of apple juice contains about twenty apples. That's a lot of apples to eat at once. Imagine munching your way through twenty apples. You would probably have tummy ache after ten, and the tummy ache is because the Poobugs have sent a message up the line to STOP EATING ANY MORE APPLES today!

That's because the poo processor only works properly when there is a nice variety. And a slow and steady stream of leftovers.
But SOMETIMES things speed up, and get completely out of control...

"Incoming apple juice!" shouted Acidophilus. "Lots of it!" The Poobugs rushed around, trying to catch the juice in their buckets, to save some for later. But soon the buckets were all full and overflowing. There was nothing to sift and sort, or chop or bash, and nothing solid to slow down the flow. Just apple juice and nothing else.

The Poobugs sloshed their buckets into the poo processor and Baxter turned the handle. It didn't groan or clang, or shudder or creak. It whizzed round like a spinning top.

The trap door opened, and a river of runny poo swooshed out towards the exit. Baxter grabbed the handle of the poo processor to hold on and then snatched at Prevotella's leg who was being swept along in a torrent of turdy gloop.

Now you might think that poo is dirty. That's what nearly everybody thinks!
But the Poobugs are the cleanest creatures you could ever hope to meet.

"A place for everything and everything in its place" is their motto.
They are meticulous in keeping their workshop spick and span,
with a sparkle and shine. After every poo they sweep and scrub.

But now all around, the Poobugs were slipping and sliding in a sloppy mess.
They needed something rough and tough to swish around the workshop to gather up the gloop and make a proper poo.

"We want green beans and broccoli!" said Liliashus.
"We want steak and sausages!" said Prevotella.

Pops thought so too, and dished up a plate of boiled cabbage and bacon.

"Eurgghh!!!" said Someone, who, when Pops wasn't looking, opened the freezer and found a great big pot of ice cream.

Very cold ice cream is delicious. But by the time it gets to your tummy the temperature is like warm milk. Sickly-sweet warm milk. Now that might work quite well mixed up with chicken and chips, or burger and baked beans. But sickly-sweet warm milk and runny apple juice?

The Poobugs do NOT like that.

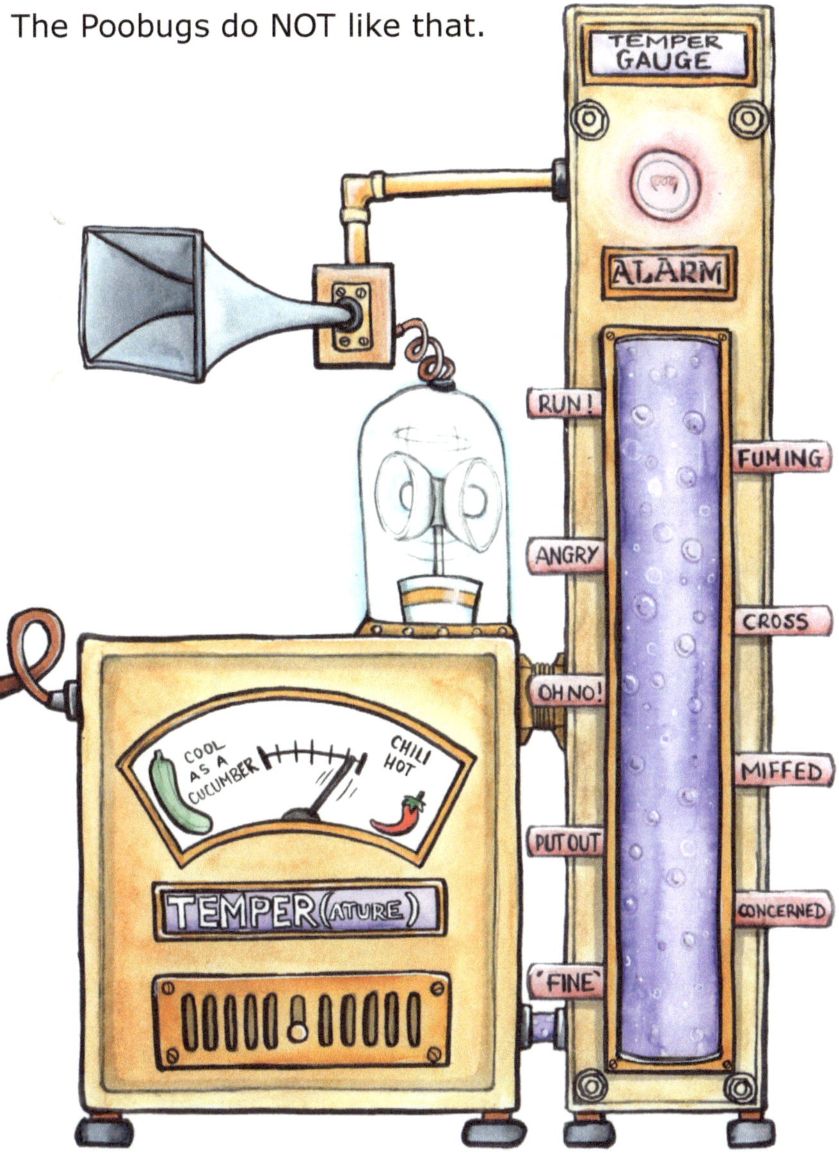

Pops was VERY cross. And Someone was very cross that Pops was cross.

So everyone was cross and there was a lot of shouting.

When people get cross and start shouting, it's sometimes said that things are 'getting heated'.

Being cross seems to make you hot. And the hotter you are outside the hotter you are inside.

Whirlygig was whizzing around,
trying to cool everything down.

But the warm milk ice cream curdled with the leftover apple juice and started to fizz.

And froth.

And bubble and pop like a saucepan of soup on the stove, about to boil over.

Normally the Tunnel of Been is ONE WAY ONLY.

Downwards.

Food goes in the top and poo comes out of the bottom.
If it was the other way around the Poo Bugs would have a much harder job!
Pushing uphill all day long. If you ate your lunch standing on your head, think what that would feel like!

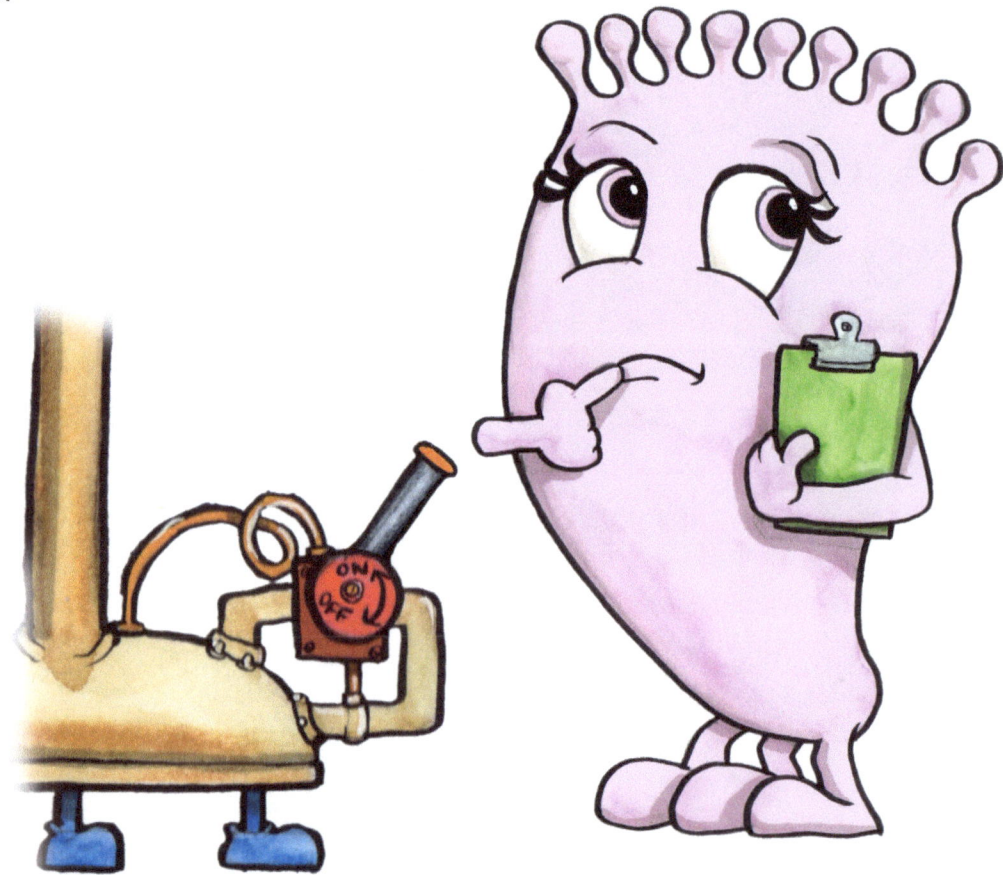

So in between the top and the bottom is Bouncer, guarding the gate to the Tunnel, and making sure everything is moving along nicely in the right direction.

But now Bouncer heard a holler from deep down below.

"Back it up! Back it up!"

Prevotella and Liliashus were hopping up and down in panic.

The volcano of soupy slop was close to erupting.

"No use crying over spilt milk apple juice", said Ruminoco, who was the quietest, calmest Poobug. The best policemen are always quiet and calm.

The best policemen also find themselves directing traffic when there has been a SERIOUS INCIDENT.

On the wall of the workshop is a big red switch.

The SERIOUS INCIDENT CONTROL KNOB.

The Poobugs are usually so good at their job, slowly sorting through the leftovers, they often forget all about the switch.

But now, there it was.

The Poobugs all stared at the switch which was labelled in big red letters S.I.C.K.

Ruminoco was the quietest, calmest Poobug,
but he could still holler with the best of them when necessary.

"Back it up!" he roared again and "hold on tight!"
Prevotella and Liliashus stopped hopping up and down and held on to each other.

Baxter took a deep breath and pushed the knob.

The Tunnel shook and rumbled, and Someone's tummy grumbled.

Bouncer flung the gate open and then……………

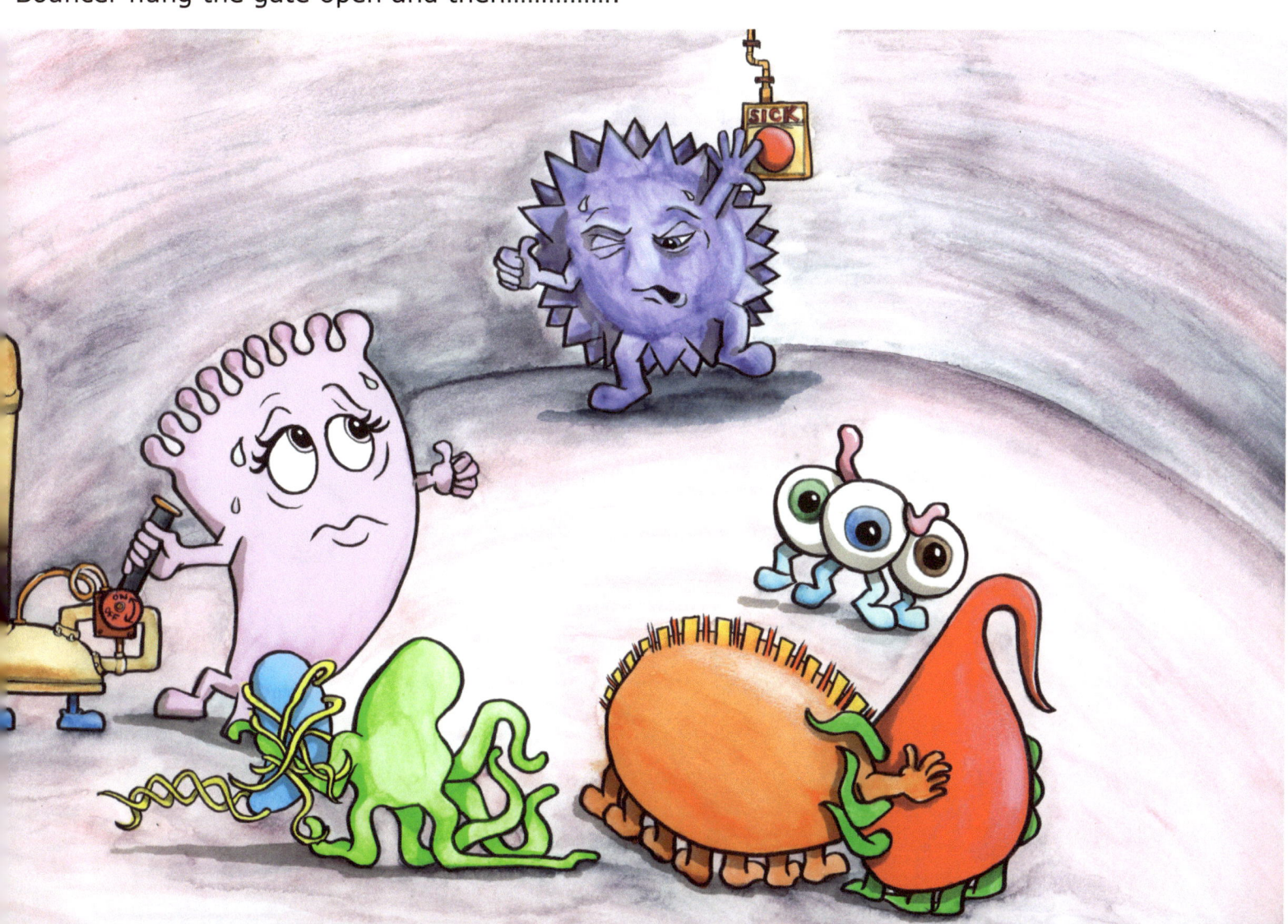

Someone was sick all over the carpet.

"Straight to bed with you!" said Pops,
wiping Someone's very hot head with a nice cool flannel.

And all day and all night Someone stayed in bed, feeling very icky.

Meanwhile, the Poobugs set to work again.

They systematically searched through the Tunnel from top to bottom, checking every nook and cranny for any last leftovers which hadn't been sent back up. And there are a LOT of nooks and crannies, winding up, round and down again.

If the Tunnel of Been was a straight line it would stretch from the top of your head almost to your toes!

They marched up and down with their buckets and brooms. They crawled into corners and wiped down the walls. And soon everywhere was spotlessly clean.

Now the Tunnel of Been was completely empty and the Poobugs had nothing to do.

But worst of all they had NOTHING TO EAT!

The Poobugs are teeny tiny creatures which means that without food they get very hungry very quickly.

It was an alarming situation.

A big fat tear rolled down Prevotella's cheek.

Bouncer carefully pushed open the gate to the Tunnel. She peeked through the crack, to see if there was anything on its way down, but it was dark and deserted.

Whirlygig tried to cheer everyone up by singing 'Let's Pretend'.
"Look! Here comes the first course,
it's chicken and chips with chocolate sauce.
Here's a banana, and now an orange……"

but she couldn't think of anything to rhyme with orange, or banana for that matter, so she flopped glumly to the floor.

But the next day Someone felt much better, and also felt absolutely famished! For two whole days Someone ate breakfast, lunch and dinner.

Pops was very strict. There was no ice cream in the freezer, no juice in the fridge.

There was porridge with raisins, egg custard with bananas, there was sweetcorn and sausages, potatoes and peas, oranges and plums.

And all washed down with lots of water.

There was a fishy trout, and even a brussel sprout. Someone threw that on the floor, but Pops picked it straight back up and put it on the plate again!
And Someone then had to stay at the table until the plate was clean.

And for two whole days nothing came out the other end. Every morning Pops called out "Have you been yet?"   Nothing. Someone felt a bit strange.

There was a lot going on in the Tunnel. There were gurgles and pops, and bubbles and squeaks. The Poobugs were happily hard at work again, chewing and chomping, sifting and sorting through the growing pile of poo-stuff. And they were taking their time.

"Sweetcorn and gristly bits!" shouted Prevotella.
"Oat flakes and orange pips!" sang Liliashus.
And Acidophilus was running back and forth with parcels of goodies galore.

Then on day three of no poo there was a long fat tube down the left side of Someone's tummy. Like an extra-large hot dog, bulging in the middle.

If you're eating what the Poobugs like best, you might sometimes feel a bulgy tube too. That's because the poo processor sits at the bottom of the left side of your tummy.

That's why, if you have a tummy ache, always rub your tummy one way, in a clockwise direction, up, round and down, to help the Poobugs push the poo-stuff along.

Baxter shovelled the poo-stuff into the poo processor.
The other Poobugs crowded round and peered over the side.

The poo-stuff was soft and squishy, like a chocolate éclair. It was shiny and brown like an autumn conker. Baxter turned the handle.
The poo processor whirred and purred, smoothly and steadily.
And out came a perfect poo.
The Poobugs felt marvellous.

And so did someone else.

www.ingramcontent.com/pod-product-compliance
Lightning Source LLC
Chambersburg PA
CBHW042250100526
44587CB00002B/81